Baby Blues® **9** Scrapbook

Check, please...

Baby Blues® **9** Scrapbook

Check, please...

By Rick Kirkman and Jerry Scott

**Andrews McMeel
Publishing**

Kansas City

Baby Blues is syndicated internationally by King Features Syndicate, Inc. For information, write King Features Syndicate, Inc., 216 East 45th Street, New York, New York 10017.

www.andrewsmcmeel.com

98 99 00 01 02 BAH 10 9 8 7 6 5 4 3 2 1

ISBN: 0-8362-5423-6

Library of Congress Catalog Card Number: 97-80774

To Tom and Marla, who have made us feel at home so quickly in our new neighborhood; to Steve and Roberto, who made my studio livable; to Katherine, Danny, Rosie, Maria, Sophie, Dylan, Michael, and teachers Shari, Janet, and Melissa, who help make Abbey's life fun; and to Kim, who in the middle of our first, and last, remodeling project, is still talking to me.
—J.S.

To Sukey, who can never be thanked enough. And to all those teachers who *didn't* tell me to stop drawing all over everything.
—R.K.

8

BABY BLUES

RICK KIRKMAN BY JERRY SCOTT

12

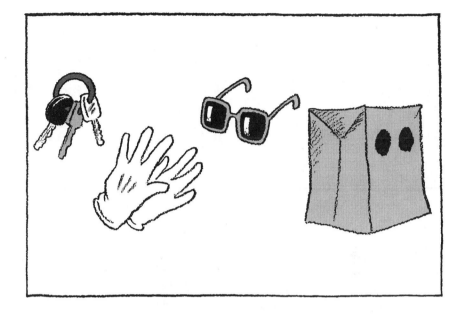

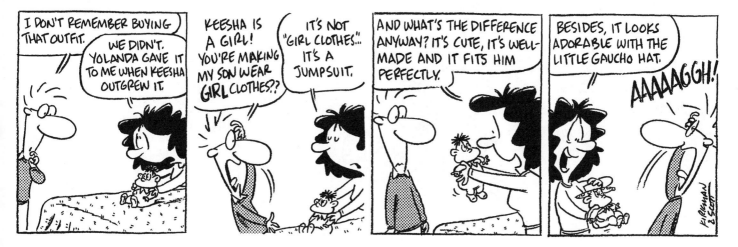

19

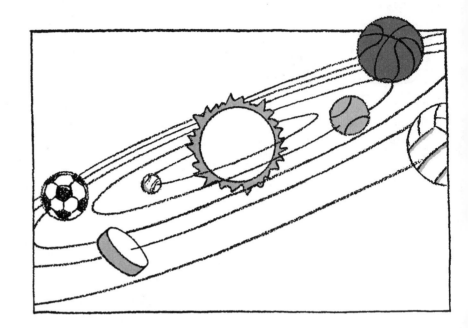

21

BABY BLUES®

BY RICK KIRKMAN / JERRY SCOTT

27

37

39

41

43

44

BABY BLUES

RICK KIRKMAN / JERRY SCOTT

TICK
TICK
TICK

51

54

60

BABY BLUES®

BY RICK KIRKMAN / JERRY SCOTT

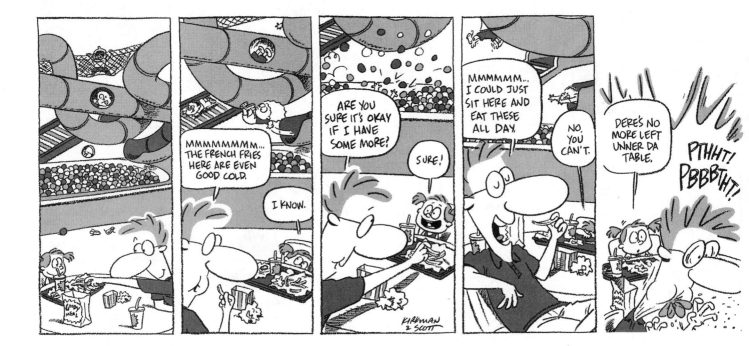

66

BABY BLUES®

BY RICK KIRKMAN / JERRY SCOTT

68

LEAKY DIAPER.

GREAT.

THERE'S NOTHING WORSE THAN CHANGING THE SHEETS ON A BED AT THREE O'CLOCK IN THE MORNING.

WAA-AAA-AAAA!

HOW ABOUT CHANGING THE SHEETS ON **TWO** BEDS AT THREE O'CLOCK IN THE MORNING?

I STAND CORRECTED.

THE END.

WEAD IT AGAIN!

COME ON, ZOE! I'VE READ "TOAD IN THE ROAD" THREE TIMES ALREADY! HOW ABOUT SOMETHING DIFFERENT?

NO! TOAD INNA WOAD! TOAD INNA WOAD!

ALL RIGHT! ALL RIGHT! YOU WIN!

SINCE WHEN DO TOADS GRIT THEIR TEETH WHEN THEY TALK?

GOOD EVENING, SIR! MY NAME IS DARRYL AND I'LL BE YOUR WAITER THIS EVENING.

TONIGHT OUR CHEF HAS PREPARED AN ENTREE I'M SURE YOU'LL FIND SATISFYING. IT IS A SINGLE COURSE, SERVED WARM, FOLLOWED BY A GENTLE BACK MASSAGE PERFORMED PERSONALLY BY THE CHEF HERSELF.

AND FOR DESSERT WE HAVE SWEET DREAMS!

ENJOY YOUR MEAL.

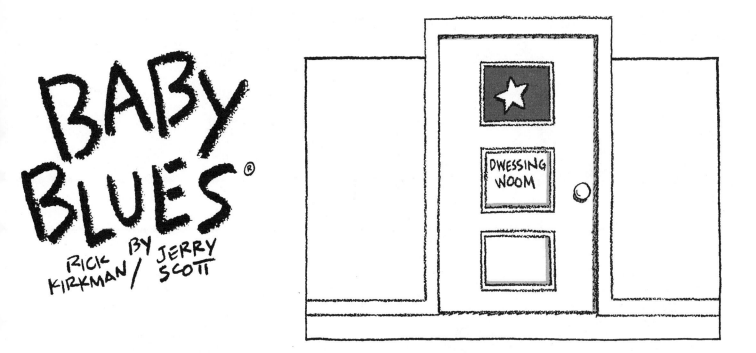

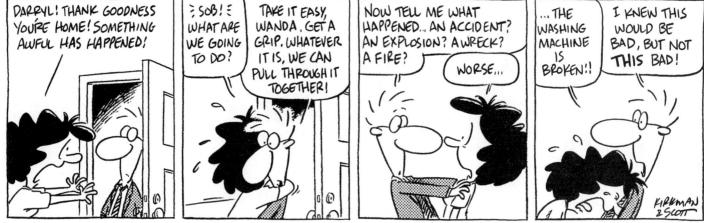

Baby Blues

by Rick Kirkman / Jerry Scott

ZOE, I'M CALLING GRANDMA ON THE PHONE...DO YOU WANT TO TALK TO HER?

BEEP! BEEP! BEEP!

NO.

OH, COME ON! JUST SAY HI TO GRANDMA,

NO!

PLEASE? JUST ONE LITTLE HI.

NO!

SHE WOULD LOVE TO HEAR YOUR VOICE, SWEETHEART! CAN YOU COUNT TO FIVE FOR GRANDMA?

NO!

WHAT ABOUT YOUR ABCs? CAN YOU SAY YOUR ABCs?

NO!

TELL GRANDMA WHAT WE HAD FOR DINNER TONIGHT WAS IT SPAGHETTI? SAY SPAGHETTI,

NO!

SORRY, MOM, I GUESS SHE'S NOT IN THE MOOD, MAYBE NEXT TIME...

CLICK!

DAT WAS FUN! LET'S CALL HER AGAIN!

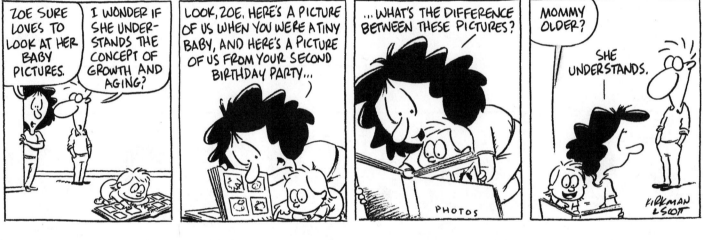

BABY BLUES®

BY RICK KIRKMAN / JERRY SCOTT

101

Panel 1: (Mother and father by the bedside)

Panel 2:
FINALLY!
THEY'RE BOTH ASLEEP!
CLICK!

Panel 3:
IT'S SO NICE WHEN THE KIDS FINALLY GET TO SLEEP SO WE CAN SIT DOWN TOGETHER AND...

Panel 4:
ZZZZZZZZZZZZZ

KIRKMAN & SCOTT

Panel 5:
OKAY, IF YOU'RE GOING TO HOLD HAMMIE IN YOUR LAP, YOU NEED TO SIT UP STRAIGHT, PUT YOUR ARM UP LIKE THIS, WITH YOUR OTHER HAND HERE...

Panel 6:
... PUT YOUR LEGS TOGETHER, REST YOUR ELBOW UP HERE, AND—WHOOPS! HAMMIE IS WET! STAY THERE AND I'LL BE RIGHT BACK.

Panel 7:
WHATCHA DOING, ZOE?
HOLDING HAMMIE.

KIRKMAN & SCOTT

Panel 8:
IS A VIVID IMAGINATION A SIGN OF HIGH INTELLIGENCE?

Panel 9:
THAT WAS LOTS OF FUN, BUT NOW IT'S TIME TO CLEAN UP OUR MESS.
WHY?

Panel 10:
BECAUSE THAT'S HOW WE TAKE CARE OF OUR THINGS.
WHY?
BECAUSE THEY STAY NICE THAT WAY.
WHY?

KIRKMAN & SCOTT

Panel 11:
BECAUSE IT... WE... YOU... UH...
BECAUSE I SAID SO!
OH.

Panel 12:
FOOLPROOF REASONING YOU HAVE THERE.
IT'S HEREDITARY.

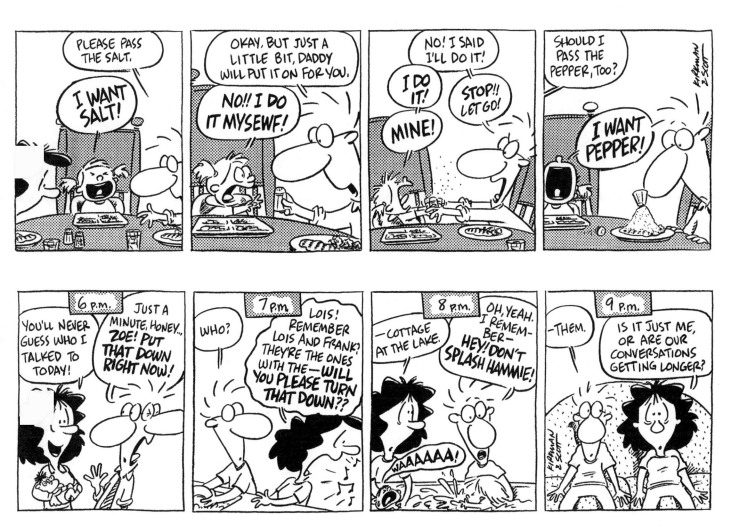

BABY BLUES®

BY RICK KIRKMAN / JERRY SCOTT

CAN YOU GET THAT, HONEY?

RING! RING!

SURE.

IT'S YOLANDA. SHE WANTS TO KNOW IF WE CAN COME OVER FOR DINNER SATURDAY.

THAT SOUNDS GREAT! ASK HER WHAT WE CAN BRING.

WHAT CAN WE BRING?

SHE SAYS WE CAN BRING EITHER A SALAD OR DESSERT.

TELL HER WE'LL BRING A SALAD.

WE'LL BRING A SALAD.

SHE WANTS TO KNOW WHAT TIME WE CAN COME OVER.

HOW ABOUT FOUR O'CLOCK?

HOW ABOUT FOUR O'CLOCK?

FOUR IS OKAY, BUT FIVE WOULD BE BETTER.

OKAY. FIVE IS FINE.

FIVE IS FINE.

SHE WANTS US TO BRING ZOE'S HIGHCHAIR.

WOULD HER BOOSTER SEAT BE OKAY INSTEAD?

WOULD HER BOOSTER SEAT BE OKAY INSTEAD?

SHE SAYS SURE, WHATEVER I THINK.

WHAT DO I THINK?

KIRKMAN & SCOTT

BABY BLUES®

RICK KIRKMAN / JERRY SCOTT BY

Panel 1: HONEY, WOULD YOU PUT THAT LOAD OF CLOTHES IN THE WASHING MACHINE FOR ME? — SURE.

Panel 2: SMALL, MEDIUM OR LARGE LOAD? — LARGE.

Panel 3: HOT, WARM OR COLD WATER? — WARM.

Panel 4: BLEACH OR NO BLEACH? — NO BLEACH!

Panel 5: LEVEL CUP OR HEAPING CUP OF DETERGENT? — I DON'T KNOW... LEVEL! IT DOESN'T MATTER! SHOULD THE SOAP GO IN **UNDER** THE CLOTHES, OR ON **TOP** OF THE CLOTHES?

Panel 6: I DON'T CARE! JUST TURN THE STUPID THING ON!!!

Panel 7: SLOSH! SLOSH!

Panel 8: ANYTHING ELSE I CAN DO TO HELP OUT, HONEY?

111

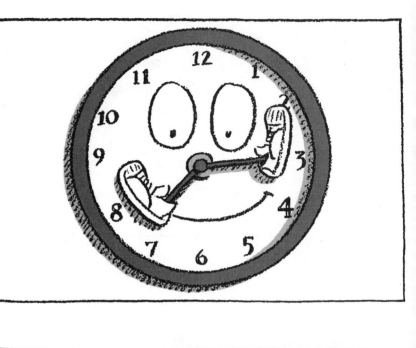

BABY BLUES

BY RICK KIRKMAN / JERRY SCOTT

THE END